MERIDIAN MIDDLE SC
2195 Brandywyn La
Buffalo Grove, IL 60089

W9-AKW-444

Cross-Training

An Integrated Life of Fitness

Core Workouts

Cross-Training

Eating Right & Additional Supplements for Fitness

Endurance & Cardio Training

Exercise for Physical & Mental Health

Flexibility & Agility

Sports & Fitness

Step Aerobics & Aerobic Dance

Weightlifting & Strength Building

Yoga & Pilates

An Integrated Life of Fitness

Cross-Training

Z.B. HILL

Mason Crest

Mason Crest
450 Parkway Drive, Suite D
Broomall, PA 19008
www.masoncrest.com

Printed and bound in the United States of America.

First printing
9 8 7 6 5 4 3 2 1

Series ISBN: 978-1-4222-3156-2
Hardcover ISBN: 978-1-4222-3158-6
Paperback ISBN: 978-1-4222-3196-8
ebook ISBN: 978-1-4222-8696-8

Cataloging-in-Publication Data on file with the Library of Congress.

CONTENTS

KEY ICONS TO LOOK FOR:

Text-Dependent Questions: These questions send the reader back to the text for more careful attention to the evidence presented there.

Words to Understand: These words with their easy-to-understand definitions will increase the reader's understanding of the text, while building vocabulary skills.

Series Glossary of Key Terms: This back-of-the book glossary contains terminology used throughout this series. Words found here increase the reader's ability to read and comprehend higher-level books and articles in this field.

Research Projects: Readers are pointed toward areas of further inquiry connected to each chapter. Suggestions are provided for projects that encourage deeper research and analysis.

Sidebars: This boxed material within the main text allows readers to build knowledge, gain insights, explore possibilities, and broaden their perspectives by weaving together additional information to provide realistic and holistic perspectives.

INTRODUCTION

Choosing fitness as a priority in your life is one of the smartest decisions you can make! This series of books will give you the tools you need to understand how your decisions about eating, sleeping, and physical activity can affect your health now and in the future.

And speaking of the future: YOU are the future of our world. We who are older are depending on you to build something wonderful—and we, as lifelong advocates of good nutrition and physical activity, want the best for you throughout your whole life.

Our hope in these books is to support and guide you to instill healthy behaviors beginning today. You are in a unique position to adopt healthy habits that will guide you toward better health right now and avoid health-related problems as an adult.

You have the power of choice today. We recognize that it's a very busy world filled with overwhelming choices that sometimes get in the way of you making wise decisions when choosing food or in being active. But no previous training or skills are needed to put this material into practice right away.

We want you to have fun and build your confidence as you read these books. Your self-esteem will increase. LEARN, EXPLORE, and DISCOVER, using the books as your very own personal guide. A tremendous amount of research over the past thirty years has proven that the quality of your health and life will depend on the decisions you make today that affect your body, mind, and inner self.

You are an individual, liking different foods, doing different things, having different interests, and growing up in different families. But you are not alone as you face these vital decisions in your life. Those of us in the fitness professions are working hard to get healthier foods into your schools; to make sure you have an opportunity to be physically active on a regular basis; to ensure that walking and biking are encouraged in your communities; and to build communities where healthy, affordable foods can be purchased close to home. We're doing all we can to support you. We've got your back!

Moving step by step to healthier eating habits and increasing physical activity requires change. Change happens in small steps, so be patient with yourself. Change takes time. But get started *now*.

Lead an "action-packed" life! Your whole body will thank you by becoming stronger and healthier. You can look and do your best. You'll feel good. You'll have more energy. You'll reap the benefits of smart lifestyle choices for a healthier future so you can achieve what's important to you.

Choose to become the best you can be!

—*Diana H. Hart, President*
National Association for Health and Fitness

Words to Understand

researchers: People who investigate the answers to various questions by doing scientific tests and studies.

effective: Able to do a job well or accomplish a goal quickly and easily.

proficiency: A skill in a particular area.

Chapter One
WHAT IS CROSS-TRAINING?

A lot of work needs to go into making a body healthy and strong. Eating right, sleeping enough, and exercising are three ways to work toward a healthy lifestyle. Consuming the right types of food and sleeping at least eight hours a night are hard enough goals to achieve, but getting out there and exercising regularly requires real time and effort.

There are a lot of benefits to exercising. Research has found that people who exercise regularly are less likely to develop heart disease and feel depressed. Regular exercise boosts the immune system, which can keep you from getting sick as often. A good, long workout has been linked to improved sleeping patterns, which is another part of maintaining a healthy lifestyle. The positive effects of exercising are just too good to pass up!

Entering the world of exercise can be intimidating at first. There are so many different exercises to choose from, and so many fitness goals to achieve. Running can help with weight loss, for example, but lifting weights can improve muscle strength. How can you choose which of them is the best exercise for you? Fortunately, you don't have to pick just one. Exercising in more than one way is actually better for the body overall.

EXERCISE PLANS

People who are new to regular exercise often make some mistakes when getting started. The first mistake they make is not exercising enough. *Researchers* have found that an exercise is not *effective* unless

Make Connections: Fitness Plateau

Athletes who focus too much on one area of fitness can reach what is referred to as a fitness plateau. Reaching this plateau means they are incapable of getting any better at the particular exercise they have been performing; they are as good as they are going to get. Reaching a fitness plateau can take months and months of strenuous exercise, but once it is reached there is really nowhere else to go. Athletes who train more than one way will never reach that plateau because they do not focus solely on one area; there is always another goal to reach. This is one more reason cross-training is a more efficient use of an athlete's time.

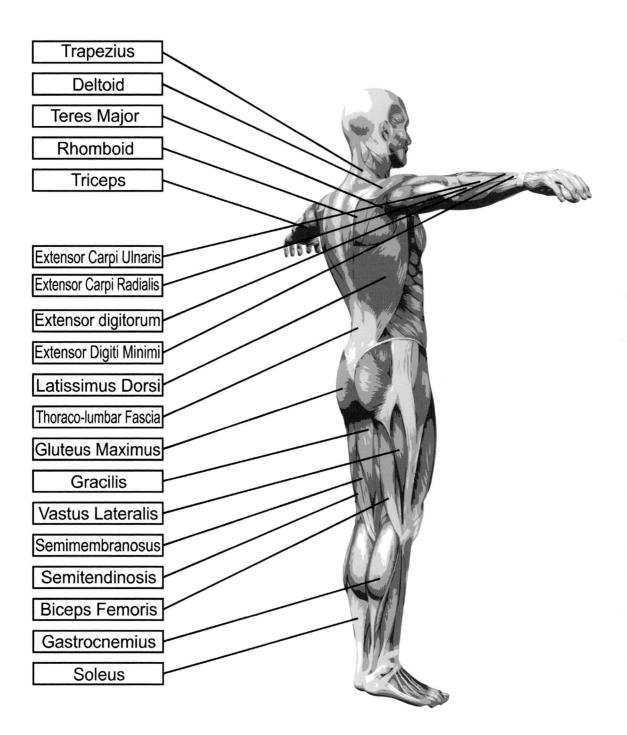

Trapezius	
Deltoid	
Teres Major	
Rhomboid	
Triceps	
Extensor Carpi Ulnaris	
Extensor Carpi Radialis	
Extensor digitorum	
Extensor Digiti Minimi	
Latissimus Dorsi	
Thoraco-lumbar Fascia	
Gluteus Maximus	
Gracilis	
Vastus Lateralis	
Semimembranosus	
Semitendinosis	
Biceps Femoris	
Gastrocnemius	
Soleus	

Your body has many groups of muscles. Cross-training is a way to exercise them all.

What Is Cross-Training?   11

performed for at least fifteen minutes with very few breaks. Exercising multiple times a week is also necessary to keep the body moving.

Another common mistake first-timers make is that they exercise too much. Muscles will become sore and swollen from being overworked. People who overwork themselves may feel so run down from a brutal routine that they stop exercising completely—and that's a step backward!

It is easy for first-timers to become discouraged while learning everything there is to know about exercise. One of the best ways to stay on top of exercising is by using an exercise plan. Exercise plans are special schedules created by a person who is knowledgeable about exercise. Following an exercise plan ensures that you are doing exactly as much exercise as you should, and no more or no less. A lot of research should be done before choosing the exercise plan that is right for you.

Exercise plans also suggest which types of exercises to perform on each day, and remind athletes of the days they need to rest during a typical exercise week. There are many different types of exercise plans, but one of the most effective is known as cross-training.

OVERALL FITNESS

Not a single exercise in the world works out every area of the body, which is why it is important to use multiple exercises to achieve overall fitness. Cross-training is a term used to describe an exercise plan that involves more than one type of exercise. The goal of cross-training is to increase overall fitness, while at the same time improving *proficiency* in one or more areas.

Performing just one exercise will not make you physically fit. There are five main components of physical fitness that must be worked on to make a body healthy and strong. They are cardiovascular endurance, muscle endurance, muscle strength, flexibility, and body composition.

Some exercises will address more than one part of physical fitness, but not a single exercise will strengthen all of them. This is why it is important to follow an exercise plan that pays attention to all five areas. Cross-training exercise plans will vary based on the athlete's ultimate goals, but every single one will include a mix of aerobic, anaerobic, and flexibility exercises. Body composition improves best through a combination of aerobic exercises and dieting.

Aerobic exercises, such as running, swimming, and cycling will strengthen the heart and lungs. A healthy cardiovascular system will have an easier time pumping blood and the oxygen it carries throughout the body. Oxygen is needed to keep the cells in the body functioning. Bodies under the strain of exercise require more oxygen than normal, forcing the heart to pump faster and work harder. Athletes with a lot of cardiovascular endurance will find it easier to keep moving for long periods of time without needing a break or feeling winded.

Anaerobic exercises do not require extra effort from the cardiovascular system. Some examples of anaerobic exercises include weight lifting and flexibility training. Athletes who spend time on muscle training will have an easier time lifting or supporting more weight on those muscles. Flexibility exercises will protect muscles from becoming stiff, sore, and injured. Stretches are one type of flexibility exercise, and yoga is another.

Many athletes start a cross-training routine with a specific goal in mind. People who play sports might want to train specific areas of the body to become even better at one sport, but this is not always the case. Some athletes use cross-training as a way to become healthier overall. Their main sport may develop only one kind of fitness, so they do cross-training in order to make their entire bodies are in shape.

PICKING PRIORITIES

People who run every day and do nothing else may be able to run long distances without getting tired—but they may not be able to lift heavy weights. Cross-training can help runners become good at all areas of physical fitness, while at the same time, the right exercises will support their dedication to running.

There are not enough hours in the day to become great at every sport in existence, and even if there were, exercising *too* much is dangerous.

The body is not capable of exercising for more time than it can handle. Cross-training allows you do a little bit of everything.

The next step is to decide what your priorities are. If you are a wrestler, for example, you might want to focus your cross-training on exercises that will help you develop agility and cardiovascular strength. If you are a swimmer, you might want to lift weights. At the same time, you'll want to include exercises that will support your main sport. Even if you're not an athlete, you can take a look at your life to see what kinds

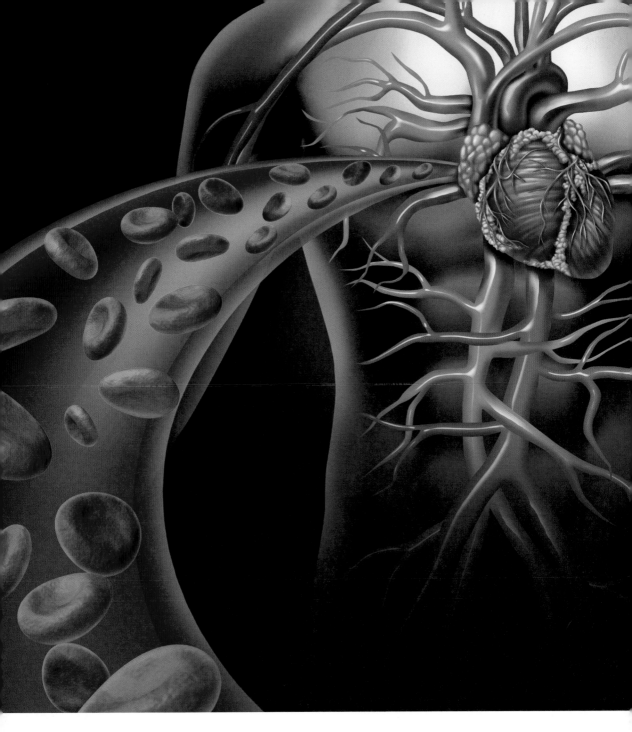

Exercises that strengthen your cardiovascular system improve the strength of your heart and blood vessels. This gets more oxygen to the muscles in your arms and legs, which means you'll be able to work out longer. Having a strong heart has many other health benefits as well.

What Is Cross-Training? 15

Some gyms offer "aerobic classes" like this one—but really, aerobic exercise is any movement that gets your heart and lungs working faster.

Text-Dependent Questions

1. According to the author, what are two mistakes people new to exercising are likely to make?
2. What is a fitness plateau and how can it be avoided?
3. What is cross-training, and how is it different from other exercise plans?
4. What are the five components of physical fitness? Name one exercise that can be used to strengthen each one.

of exercise you need most. If you do a lot of babysitting, for example, that means you're always running around with little kids, you might want to work on developing your upper-body strength. Or if you have a job where you do a lot of lifting, you might want to focus on running or some other aerobic exercise. Deciding on the perfect plan is the first step toward pursing it!

Words to Understand

tendons: The stretchy bands that connect muscles to bones.
buoyancy: The ability to float.
evolutionary: Having to do with the natural process by which biological characteristics are changed as inherited material is passed from generation to generation.

Chapter Two

WHAT ARE THE BENEFITS OF CROSS-TRAINING?

While the direct physical benefits of these exercises are many, there are also a number of other benefits that are not as obvious. Cross-training benefits athletes in ways that other exercise plans do not. A decreased risk of injury, the ability to keep exercising even when injured, and the option to exercise in any type of weather are just a few of the ways athletes can benefit from a cross-training platform.

Make Connections: More Than Just Fitness

Becoming physically fit is just one of the many reasons to exercise. Martial artists learn how to defend themselves through extensive physical training, while at the same time strengthening their body and mind. For this reason, cross-training in martial arts takes on a whole new meaning. Mixed martial arts instructors teach their students many different self-defense techniques while at the same forcing them to develop every component of physical fitness.

DECREASED RISK OF INJURY

The human body is not a machine. As humans exercise, strain is placed on the joints, muscles, and *tendons*. Without proper rest, muscles and joints can get worn down and injured through repeated use. Runners will hurt their joints and leg muscles if they aren't careful. Weight trainers could suffer a muscle tear or strain if they push themselves too hard or too fast.

Injuries that occur due to exercising a certain body part too much are known as overuse injuries. Athletes must pay special attention to their exercise plans if they are to avoid overuse injuries. Cross-training naturally reduces the risk of overuse injuries because it encourages athletes to perform varied exercises throughout the week, giving the muscles and joints a day or two to rest before they are exercised once more.

Another way cross-training directly prevents injury is by paying attention to every single area of physical fitness. Endurance, strength, and flexibility all improve at a steady rate, which reduces the likelihood of certain areas of the body becoming weak while others grow very

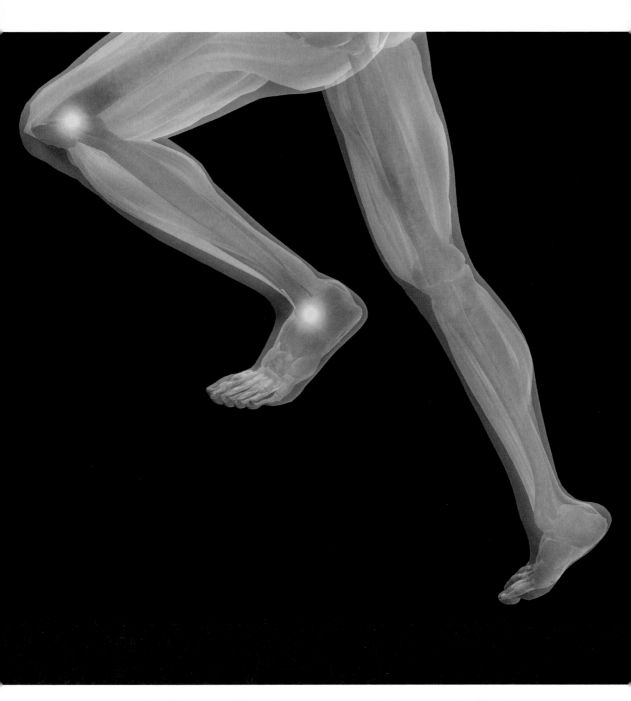

Your joints get a lot of wear and tear during exercise. The knees and ankles, for example, are the places that absorb most of the impact from running.

What Are the Benefits of Cross-Training?

strong. For example, people who only run are prone to having very strong leg muscles but noticeably weak arms. Runners might believe they are physically fit because of how often they exercise, but they are actually more likely to become injured due to the imbalance in their muscle strengths.

Cross-training naturally balances the muscle groups of the body, while also improving endurance and flexibility. In a runner's case, cross-training will improve the arm muscles, giving the athlete a better chance at preventing all types of injury.

KEEP MOVING

Even the best athletes can still get hurt, though, and the best way to repair an injured body part is to give it time to rest. Athletes who usually exercise regularly may feel disappointed and even restless when they are told by a doctor that they should not train at the same level they did before the injury. Fortunately, they don't have to stop training completely if they use a cross-training exercise plan!

One of the benefits of cross-training is that you can continue to exercise even when you are forced to give certain areas of the body a rest. A runner who injures his leg while exercising will still be able to strengthen his arm muscles by lifting weights or doing pushups. Someone with a sprained wrist can safely jog on a treadmill while waiting for the injury to heal.

Cross-training offers plenty of options to athletes who are recovering from injury. Easing an injured muscle back into action becomes easier with the right exercises. Swimming is one way to strengthen muscles when they are weaker than normal. The *buoyancy* of water will put less strain on muscles and joints. Athletes who are not yet ready to put their full weight on an injured muscle can use time in the pool as a half-way point between being injured and being well.

NEVER STOP EXERCISING!

Even athletes who aren't injured or sick still have to deal with the weather! It's not safe to exercise outside in very cold or hot weather,

Runners who've hurt a knee joint or leg muscle may find doing push-ups a good change of pace while they recover.

What Are the Benefits of Cross-Training? 23

Exercise can help you keep a positive attitude and feel better about yourself. In addition to a healthier body, better sleep, and more energy, regular exercise can also help you smile more!

and being outside during a thunderstorm or snowstorm can be dangerous no matter what the temperature is. Some areas of the world make it nearly impossible to exercise outside for months at a time due to the weather, and active athletes in these locations must find alternatives to their normal routine.

Make Connections: Keep It Interesting!

 Performing the same exercise day in and day out can get pretty boring. Cross-training prevents that boredom by offering a wide array of different exercises you can perform. Each component of physical fitness can be improved in different ways. Athletes who feel engaged and excited about exercising are more likely to stick to an exercise plan than athletes that grow tired of the same routine day in and day out.

Cross-training plans offer options for days when going outside simply isn't an option. Cyclists who spend most of their time outside, for instance, could feel forced to just skip a day of exercise during bad weather, but a cyclist who follows a cross-training plan can simply replace his usual cycling routine with another endurance exercise without skipping a beat. Aerobic exercises such as running on a treadmill or swimming in an indoor pool can be substituted for cycling without the need to actually go outside.

MENTAL BENEFITS

All forms of exercise affect the body and mind in a positive way, and cross-training is no different. The natural high of feeling fit and ready to take on the world is not just a mental interpretation; it is a chemical reaction. The human body releases special chemicals during and after exercise known as hormones. These hormones are responsible for the way an athlete feels after a great workout session.

One of the most well-known hormones released during exercise is adrenaline. This chemical comes from the adrenal gland, and it actually serves a very important *evolutionary* purpose. Before the safety of modern technology, humans relied on something known as the fight-or-flight reflex. Adrenaline was pumped into the body to give humans an extra burst of energy in situations where they truly needed it. This extra energy would help them fight off an attacker or flee from a dangerous situation. Today, adrenaline serves a slightly different purpose. Repeated exercise can cause the body to become tired, and adrenaline is there to help the body push through that fatigue.

Another important chemical released into the body during exercise is endorphins. These are sometimes referred to as chemical rewards for exercising. In other words, they make the body feel good both during and after exercise, increasing the likelihood that an athlete will exercise again. Endorphins are released by the pituitary gland. They can help an athlete become relaxed after a hard day of working out.

CROSS-TRAINING FOR SPORTS

Sports are more than just a fun way to stay active. They are an effective form of exercise, too! Many sports focus on one area of physical fitness, but not the others. Soccer players, for example, will run around a lot and kick a ball down the field, but they don't use their arm muscles very often. Their shins and feet get used very often, but may weaken over time from repeated use and lack of strength exercises.

Cross-training for soccer players would involve a lot of arm exercises to make the body well-rounded. Soccer players would also have to pay special attention to the muscles they use regularly on the field. It is easy to injure a body part that isn't exercised regularly, even if it is used frequently in a sports game. Calf and foot exercises will help strengthen a soccer player's muscles and tendons to reduce the risk of injury.

The extra exercises athletes perform off the field will help to boost their performance in a game, giving them an advantage over other players who do not take the time to exercise regularly when they aren't playing a sport. Many sports coaches and personal trainers encourage their players to exercise regularly, even during the off-season.

If you have an injured muscle or joint, swimming allows you to continue to get aerobic exercise while not putting stress on the injury.

What Are the Benefits of Cross-Training? 27

Research Project

Using the Internet, research a sport you are interested in and explain which areas of physical fitness this sport exercises and which areas it neglects. Then, research cross-training exercises designed specifically for this sport. What are some suggested cross-training exercises for an athlete who plays this particular sport, and why are they important?

Cross-training is a good way for a wrestler to work on other forms of fitness besides the muscle strength he needs for wrestling. He might want to lift weights to strengthen his muscles for his sport, while also running or doing some other form of aerobic exercise to build his cardiovascular fitness.

Text-Dependent Questions

1. What are overuse injuries and how can cross-training prevent them?
2. Why can athletes who injure themselves continue to exercise while using a cross-training program?
3. What type of external variables, besides illness and injury, might prevent an athlete from exercising? Explain how cross-training deals with these variables.
4. Explain what adrenaline and endorphins are and how they assist in the act of exercising.
5. How can cross-training improve how an athlete performs in sports?

When a sporting season is over, athletes used to exercising on a daily basis will have no trouble staying in shape while waiting for the next season to begin. Sports athletes who don't exercise regularly, on the other hand, may have a tough time getting back into the game when the season starts again.

Words to Understand

 core: The center part of the body, the trunk or torso.

Chapter Three

EXAMPLES OF CROSS-TRAINING WORKOUT SCHEDULES

Deciding to follow a cross-training exercise plan is a great first step to becoming more physically fit. For a lot of beginner athletes, though, it can be hard to know where to begin. Fortunately, there are many different workout schedules to choose from. This chapter contains three sample weekly schedules, along with explanations for why an athlete might choose each one.

Make Connections: Rest

 All athletes, no matter how physically fit, should take time to rest. At least one day a week should be reserved for complete and total relaxation. Another day can be used for stretches to reduce stiffness. The body needs some time to recover from all the strenuous activity it has been involved in over the past week. The sample exercise plans in this chapter include two days of rest.

Although there are five areas of physical fitness, types of exercises are usually split into three groups: aerobic exercises, anaerobic exercises, and flexibility exercises. All cross-training workout schedules spend some time focused on each area, although the particular exercises used may be changed depending on an individual's needs and future goals.

SPECIFIC GOALS

All athletes are different, and so every person's exercise plan will be unique. There are two large variables when building cross-training plans.

The first variable is how often an athlete will exercise each day. This variable is affected by how much free time an athlete has and how physically fit her body already is. People who are just beginning a new exercise plan should start off slowly. Pushing the body too hard too fast will only result in injury.

The next part of an exercise plan is the specific exercises that will be performed—and how often. Athletes training for a triathlon might spend

Yoga is a great way to build flexibility.

Examples of Cross-Training Workout Schedules

Stretching your muscles gets them ready to exercise.

Cross-Training

most of their time on endurance exercises such as running, cycling, and swimming because triathlons test athletes' overall endurance. Wrestlers are more likely to spend their time on strength-building exercises like weight training, pushups, pull-ups, and sit-ups. Gymnasts will spend a lot of their time on stretches because they are required to flex their bodies a lot while performing a gymnastic routine.

Athletes who play sports should consider their sports schedule when creating a cross-training schedule. If you run for an hour while playing a basketball game, that counts as cardio exercise.

WARMING UP

Warm-up exercises are considered by many athletes to be just as important as the main exercise itself. Every type of exercise should begin with stretches targeting every general area of the body. These warm-up stretches should also include stretches that target specific locations that will be used the most during the main exercise.

Warming up is not just a figurative term for getting ready for an exercise; it is also literal! The muscles and tendons become warm after they have been used. This heat makes them more flexible. Muscles are usually tight and stiff before being exercised, and are more likely to tear if they are not stretched prior to continued movement. Stretches technically count as flexibility exercises, so performing them helps address that area of overall fitness.

Easing into an exercise is the best way to get the body ready for an intense workout. If you will be running, start out with a slow jog. Swimmers should take it easy during the first few laps around the pool. Strength training should begin with lighter weights, and slowly build up to the heaviest weight with which the athlete is comfortable.

COOLING DOWN

Like warming up, cooling down is extremely important and should never be skipped. The process of cooling down should occur in multiple steps,

Make Connections: Too Much Training!

 One of the biggest questions beginner athletes might ask is when they should increase training. Thirty minutes of exercise each day is not a lot, especially for someone who is used to that amount of activity. As a general rule, athletes should not increase the amount of exercise they do by more than 10 percent per week. Until they are absolutely comfortable with the increase in exercise, they should not increase their workout any more than that. This means that if you've been exercising for 30 minutes at a time, you should only push that up to 33 minutes the first week that you increase your time. The following week, you could go up to 36 minutes, and the week after that, 40 minutes. In general, athletes should never exercise more than 90 minutes per day, and this should only occur when training for an upcoming competition. Athletes who train this much will have to compensate for the long sessions by taking more days to rest each week.

with the first step being a less intense version of the main activity. If you were running, slow down to a jog and then a brisk walk. After a few minutes of that, move on to the stretching part of the cool-down.

Stretching after an exercise serves a different purpose from the stretches that occurred while warming up. The body builds up lactic acid over the course of exercising. That lactic acid is actually a good thing when it is first released into the muscles; it provides the muscles with added energy when they need it, but lactic acid buildup can cause the muscles to become sore and tense over the next few days if athletes aren't careful. Stretching following a workout is just one of the ways an athlete can reduce the soreness that can be experienced due to lactic acid.

Crunches are a good way to build core strength.

Examples of Cross-Training Workout Schedules

A BALANCED SCHEDULE

A completely balanced cross-training schedule will contain three days of aerobic exercise, two days of strength training, and one day of flexibility training. One day is reserved completely for rest. Here is one example:

- Monday: 30 minutes of aerobic exercises (5 minutes warm-up and cool-down)
- Tuesday: 30 minutes of strength training (5 minutes cardio warm-up)
- Wednesday: Rest (light stretching and flexibility exercises)
- Thursday: 30 minutes of aerobic exercises (5 minutes warm-up and cool-down)
- Friday: 30 minutes of strength training (5 minutes cardio warm-up)
- Saturday: 30 minutes of aerobic training (5 minutes warm-up and cool-down)
- Sunday: Rest

The descriptions of the types of exercise that needs to be performed each day are left vague on purpose. Athletes looking to keep their exercise routine interesting might choose to perform a different aerobic exercise on each aerobic day, but people training for a more specific purpose will probably be a little more picky about their choices.

Most cross-training exercises are used for one of two purposes. Either they are meant to improve certain muscle groups in a different way, or they are meant to balance out a muscle group that is not usually exercised. Sometimes, cross-training exercises fulfill both purposes at once!

Swimmers use a lot of upper body strength while swimming, but swimming all the time can cause overuse injuries or simply become boring! One way to train upper body strength while not in the pool is to lift heavy weights or rock climb. Runners, on the other hand, might use swimming to improve upper body strength because runners naturally do not have a lot of upper-body strength. This is an example of cross-training being used in an attempt to balance out the body's overall fitness.

FOCUSING ON CARDIO

Athletes who are more focused on cardiovascular exercises can spend more days a week performing them. While the balanced schedule featured three days of cardio, this schedule features four days of aerobic exercise. One of the strength-training days has been dropped to make room for the extra cardio day. The two days of rest have remained the same.

- Monday: 30 minutes of aerobic exercises (5 minutes warm-up and cool-down)
- Tuesday: 30 minutes of aerobic exercises (5 minutes warm-up and cool-down)
- Wednesday: Rest (light stretching and flexibility exercises)
- Thursday: 30 minutes of aerobic exercises (5 minutes warm-up and cool-down)
- Friday: 30 minutes of strength training (5 minutes cardio warm-up)
- Saturday: 30 minutes of aerobic training (5 minutes warm-up and cool-down)
- Sunday: Rest

The cardio exercises performed on Monday and Tuesday should be different from each other because performing different exercises on each day will prevent overuse injury. Running on Monday and swimming on Tuesday would be a good use of these two days. Running puts strain on the legs and joints, while swimming puts strain on the arms and shoulders. Swimming is generally easier on the joints than running, so that is why swimming would ideally occur on the day after running.

People who prefer a cardio-heavy cross-training schedule are usually focusing on a sport or exercise that requires a lot of cardiovascular endurance. Most triathlons focus on swimming, cycling, and running, which are all very cardio-heavy exercises. Someone training for a triathlon will want to become strong in all three, making a cardio-heavy exercise schedule ideal.

Examples of Cross-Training Workout Schedules   39

Lifting weights strengthens the muscles in your arms and shoulders.

Cross-Training

Choosing the right weights for you is an important part of lifting to increase your strength while avoiding injury.

FOCUSING ON STRENGTH

Athletes who put more emphasis on muscle strength should spend more days of the week exercising that area of fitness. This schedule is very similar to the balanced schedule, except Saturday has been changed to a strength-training day. The reason two strength days occur before a total rest day is to give the body time to recover after an extensive workout.

- Monday: 30 minutes of aerobic exercises (5 minutes warm-up and cool-down)

- Tuesday: 30 minutes of strength training (5 minute cardio warm-up)
- Wednesday: Rest (light stretching and flexibility exercises)
- Thursday: 30 minutes of aerobic exercises (5 minutes warm-up and cool-down)
- Friday: 30 minutes of strength training (5 minutes cardio warm-up)
- Saturday: 30 minutes of strength training (5 minutes cardio warm-up)
- Sunday: Rest

There are many different types of strength exercises. Weight lifting, for example, is very different from *core* strength training. Push-ups, pull-ups, and sit-ups are good core exercises, and they can all be performed with few if any tools or equipment. These exercises will work out the body's ability to support itself while moving. The abdomen and chest will benefit more from these exercises, while weight lifting will affect the arm and leg muscles more. Core training could occur on Friday, with weight lifting taking place on Saturday.

Text-Dependent Questions

1. What are the two main variables that should be considered when creating an exercise schedule?
2. Why is warming up so important and what might happen if an athlete doesn't warm up?
3. How can cool-down exercises reduce lactic acid buildup?
4. How many days of cardio are suggested in the balanced schedule?
5. What are two different cardio exercises that can be performed back-to-back without the risk of overuse injury?
6. What are two strength training exercises that can be performed back-to-back without the risk of overuse injury?

Strength training is an important part of any athlete's fitness, but it is more important for people who compete in areas that focus on strength. Wrestling, sprinting, and weight lifting all require a lot of muscle strength and endurance. How much focus should be spent on core training depends on exactly what the athlete is looking to get out of the cross-training.

Words to Understand

sustained: Continued without stopping.

modify: Change in some way.

aggravate: Make worse.

physical therapist: A person who is trained to help people reduce pain in their joints and muscles, while improving or getting back their ability to move easily.

asthma: Chronic breathing difficulties.

Chapter Four

CROSS-TRAINING SAFETY

C ross-training—like all types of exercise—will make the body stronger and healthier. However, some risks always come with all types of exercise. The best way to reduce these risks is by taking countermeasures to prevent any problems that might arise. Obeying the body's needs, wearing protective equipment, and resting after an injury are just three ways to stay safe during cross-training.

Make Connections: Personal Trainers

Personal fitness trainers serve many purposes. When you hire a personal fitness trainer, you are paying her for her experience and guidance. She can teach you how to exercise properly and safely while reducing the risk of injury. If you ever do get injured, she will know exactly what to do. Even if she isn't around when you are exercising, her advice will get you on the right track. Coaches serve the same purpose for people who play sports.

One of the best ways to stay safe while cross-training is to be sure you are exercising properly! Improper form can lead to injury and a whole array of other problems. A person who does not run properly is more likely to irritate his joints and muscle tissue than someone who is running correctly.

Athletes who have perfect form can exercise harder and for more time without worrying about injury. Ask a coach, personal trainer, or other experienced athlete exactly how an exercise should be done before trying it. The Internet is another great resource for exercise safety. Many websites will even mention the common mistakes athletes will make when trying a new exercise.

No one can become physically fit overnight. It takes a lot of time and hard work to get to the level of people who have been exercising for years, and there's no shame in taking it slow! Many exercise plans suggest starting off with an overall fitness evaluation so that you understand the exact condition of your body before beginning a new exercise plan.

General physical fitness evaluations test all parts of physical fitness, and the results can be surprising. Runners who have a lot of

A personal trainer can show you the best way to exercise without getting hurt.

Cross-Training Safety

No matter what kind of exercise you're doing, it's important to drink plenty of water.
Dehydration—when your body doesn't have enough water—can be very dangerous.

Cross-Training

Make Connections: Dehydration

 About 60 percent of the body is made up of water, and a lot of that water is used during exercise. It is easy to become dehydrated while exercising if you aren't careful. Remember: if you are thirsty, that means you are already slightly dehydrated. Symptoms of severe dehydration include dizziness, fatigue and nausea. If you ever experience any of these symptoms, stop exercising right away and drink a lot of water!

cardiovascular endurance but not enough muscle strength will see first-hand that they are not completely physically fit. Examining the results of a fitness evaluation both before and after a few months of cross-training exercises will show just how important cross-training can be.

THE IMPORTANCE OF FUELING

All athletes need three important things before exercising: food, water, and sleep. Keeping some food and water on hand during an exercise isn't a bad idea, either. Water is used during exercise to keep the body cool through sweating, while food is used to fuel the body and give it the energy it needs to keep going.

Merely eating a full meal before exercising isn't enough. The food that is eaten needs to be the right type of food, too. Carbohydrates—complex sugars—give athletes *sustained* energy that will keep them going throughout hours of activity. Simple sugars, on the other hand, will give athletes a quick burst of energy. Three examples of carbohydrates are bread, cereal, and pasta. Simple sugars can be found in candy, fruits, and desserts. At least 50 percent of a meal eaten before a

Playing sports is a great way to get active and stay fit, but no matter what sport you play or activity you do, make sure you have the right safety equipment.

workout should contain carbohydrates. Another important type of food to consume before exercise is anything containing protein. Proteins support muscle growth and muscle recovery. They can be found in meat and beans.

Getting enough sleep is just as important as eating right because sleeping is the time when the body recovers and heals itself. Not sleeping enough could result in a body becoming fatigued before a workout even begins, and will increase the risk of injury. People who do not sleep enough are also more likely to get sick.

PROTECTION

Some exercises require extra equipment, while others do not. Most of the equipment that is used during exercise is for the athlete's own protection. Wearing a helmet while cycling, for example, is one way to reduce the risk of head injury during a fall. Even the most experienced cyclists will wear a helmet because they know better than anyone that accidents are always a risk.

Some exercises put more strain on certain parts of the body than others. Running and jumping are hard on the knees, which is why some runners will wear knee braces even if they aren't injured. The braces give the knees extra support just in case they get tired. Braces are used in all types of sports and exercise. Bowlers might use wrist braces, while weight lifters are likely to use back braces during heavy lifting.

Padding is needed during sports where players are likely to interact with another person or object. Soccer players wear protection on their shins to protect those areas from injury as they kick the ball around a field. Football players wear full-body and shoulder padding because they run and bash into other players dozens of times during a typical football game. This padding also protects against injury from falls, which happen quite often during a tackle. Mouth guards are required for many sports because teeth are very fragile, especially in a high-impact game.

One of the most important pieces of protection an athlete can get is a good pair of shoes. All of us move around on our feet, whether we are runners, weight trainers, or people who do not exercise at all. The right shoes can also help with posture—and having proper posture is an important part of keeping the body aligned and comfortable. Proper shoes also make it easier to move without injuring the ankle or foot.

Some of the equipment used during exercise has nothing to do with safety directly. Instead, it may be a way to monitor how much the body is exercising. Pedometers keep track of how many steps are taken, while a stopwatch keeps track of time. Runners can use these tools to estimate how much and how long they have been running, which is an important part of making sure they aren't overdoing it.

INJURY

There are two major types of injury where exercising is involved: chronic injury and acute injury.

Chronic injuries are injuries that never go away or that periodically come back again and again. One type of chronic injury is overuse injury. Overuse injuries should never happen to an athlete who is properly following a cross-training exercise plan, but even the best athletes can push themselves too far.

Acute injuries happen suddenly. Three examples of acute injures are sprains, muscle tears, and bone fractures. Athletes can take certain steps to avoid acute injuries, but sometimes accidents happen no matter how much you do to try to prevent them. It is best to stop exercising and consult medical attention immediately when a serious acute injury occurs.

Not all acute injuries are serious, though. Scrapes and bruises from a fall aren't likely to keep an athlete from exercising, and they can be easily treated within the home. An icepack can be used to reduce swelling on a fresh bruise. Even the smallest cuts can become serious, though, if they get infected, so not a single injury should be ignored, no matter how small. Every person, whether an athlete or not, should keep a first aid kit handy.

The good news is that many minor injuries won't stop athletes from their ability to cross-train. Athletes will just need to be creative with how they spend their energy and perhaps *modify* their existing schedule to fit the new exercises they can perform even with their injury. Athletes who are unsure if a cross-training exercise will *aggravate* an existing injury should ask their doctor or *physical therapist* before doing it.

Some injuries are so serious that an athlete is better off not exercising

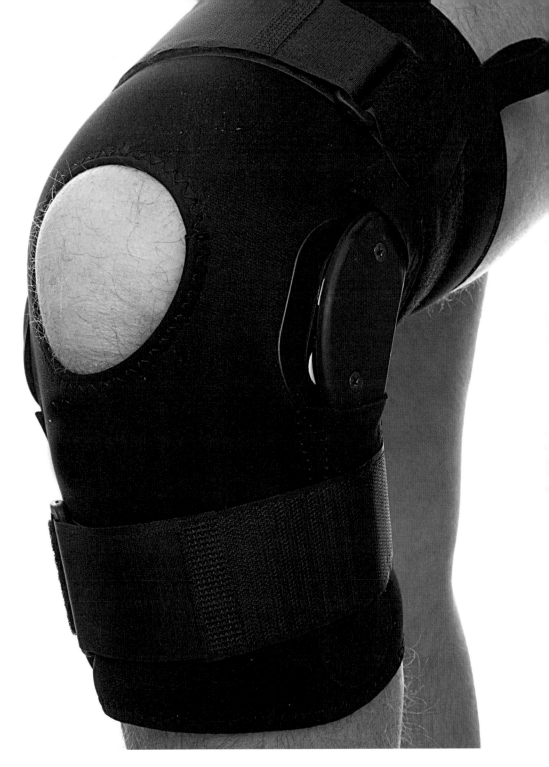

Wearing braces like this while you run is a good way to protect your knees from injury.

at all while recovering, and these usually include broken bones. It is very hard and dangerous to exercise with a cast on one of your limbs! Fortunately, cross-training can be a great way to get back on your feet after your doctor gives you the approval to exercise again. However, you should never start with the full exercise routine you were following before you became injured in the first place. Start off slow, and don't forget the importance of warm-up and cool-down stretching.

Getting injured and needing to take a long rest is like stepping backward when it comes to physical fitness. Muscle strength and cardiovascular endurance will weaken if not used repeatedly, and athletes who are forced to take a long break will be unable to keep up with their previous exercise plan. Weakened muscles are more likely to become injured, and that is the last thing you want to happen when you have taken so much time allow an injury to heal in the first place! This is why after a major injury, athletes need to be patient and be willing to start over from the beginning.

ILLNESS

Minor sicknesses like a cold are not a reason to stop exercising, but major illnesses are. The body's immune system becomes weakened as it fights off illness, which makes it even easier to pick up other sicknesses from other people and harder for the body to fight them off. Some illnesses have side effects that automatically make exercising harder, such as making it more difficult to breathe. Cardiovascular exercises are not easy for a person who cannot run far due to an illness.

The strength of muscles will also not be at their fullest when someone is sick. General body fatigue will make it harder to muster up the energy to exercise, and pushing yourself can lengthen or worsen the extent of the illness. In this case, it is best to wait until you are better to start exercising again. During minor illnesses, however, athletes simply reduce the amount they train to give their body ample time to rest and recover.

Chronic illnesses are very different from temporary illnesses in that they do not go away within just a few weeks. *Asthma*, for example,

Stretching is even more important after recovering from an injury and starting to work out again. Make sure to stretch before and after workouts.

can last for years and may never fully disappear. Some people are also prone to more joint problems than others. Arthritis is just one example of a disease that negatively affects the joints, and exercising with arthritis can be quite painful without assistance.

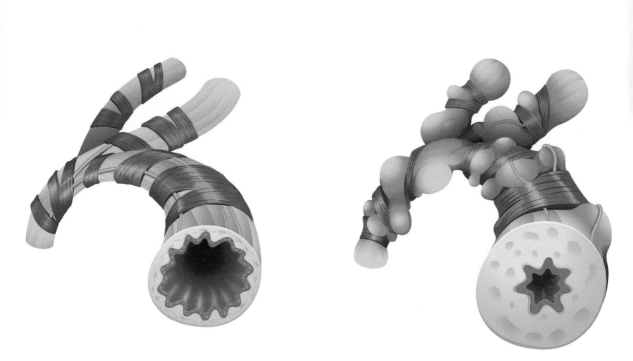

If a person has asthma, the tubes inside her lungs can become swollen, as shown in this diagram. When that happens, it's hard for her to suck air in and out of her lungs. When a person who has asthma exercises, he needs to be careful and always have any medication he needs on hand—but asthma needn't stop him from becoming a strong athlete!

Text-Dependent Questions

1. What is the purpose of an overall fitness evaluation?
2. What are the three types of "fuel" an athlete needs to stay energized?
3. How do carbohydrates and protein help an athlete prepare for a day of working out? List three types of food that contain carbohydrates and three types of food that contain protein.
4. What are three types of protective gear an athlete might wear while exercising, and what injury does each type of gear prevent?
5. Explain the difference between acute and chronic injury. What causes overuse injury and how can it be prevented?
6. How does an acute illness affect an athlete's overall ability to perform?
7. Is it possible for someone with a chronic illness to exercise? Explain why or why not.

Just because someone has a chronic illness, though, doesn't mean they can't exercise—but they should take extra steps to prepare themselves for it. People who experience chronic illnesses should consult a doctor before getting started. An overall physical examination can determine what the body can handle, and a medical professional will be able to give advice regarding which exercise plan to follow. The world of medicine has come far, and there are many remedies to the problems people with chronic illnesses face.

Basically, cross-training is a great option for pretty much anyone who wants to build fitness. Whether you're an athlete or just someone who wants to get in shape, cross-training is definitely something you should consider!

FIND OUT MORE

In Books

Bounds, Laura, Kirsten Brekken Shea, Dottiedee Agnor, and Gayden Darnell. *Health & Fitness: A Guide to a Healthy Lifestyle.* Dubuque, Iowa: Kendall Hunt, 2012.

Brown, Lee E., and Vance Ferrigno. *Training for Speed, Agility, and Quickness.* Champaign, Ill.: Human Kinetics, 2005.

Lancaster, Scott B., and Radu Teodorescu. *Athletic Fitness for Kids.* Champaign, Ill.: Human Kinetics, 2008.

Ryan, Tony, and Martica K. Heaner. *Cross-Training for Dummies.* Foster City, Calif.: IDG Worldwide, 2000.

Stewart, Brett, and Jason Warner. *Functional Cross Training: The Revolutionary, Routine-busting Approach to Total Body Fitness.* Berkeley, Calif.: Ulysses, 2014.

Online

Cross Training Improves Fitness and Reduces Injury
sportsmedicine.about.com/od/tipsandtricks/a/Cross_Training.htm

Getting Stronger and Leaner with Cross Training
www.webmd.com/fitness-exercise/features/get-stronger-and-leaner-with-cross-training

How to Maintain Fitness While Injured
sportsmedicine.about.com/od/tipsandtricks/a/TrainThruInjury.htm

Injury Prevention—Cross Training
www.coreconcepts.com.sg/mcr/injury-prevention-cross-training

Seven Cross-Training Exercises For Runners
www.active.com/running/articles/7-cross-training-exercises-for-runners

SERIES GLOSSARY OF KEY TERMS

abs: Short for abdominals. The muscles in the middle of your body, located over your stomach and intestines.

aerobic: A process by which energy is steadily released using oxygen. Aerobic exercise focuses on breathing and exercising for a long time.

anaerobic: When lots of energy is quickly released, without using oxygen. You can't do anaerobic exercises for a very long time.

balance: Your ability to stay steady and upright.

basal metabolic rate: How many calories your body burns naturally just by breathing and carrying out other body processes.

bodybuilding: Exercising specifically to get bigger, stronger muscles.

calories: The units of energy that your body uses. You get calories from food and you use them up when you exercise.

carbohydrates: The foods that your body gets most of its energy from. Common foods high in carbohydrates include sugars and grains.

cardiovascular system: Your heart and blood vessels.

circuit training: Rapidly switching from one exercise to another in a cycle. Circuit training helps build endurance in many different muscle groups.

circulatory system: The system of blood vessels in your body, which brings oxygen and nutrients to your cells and carries waste products away.

cool down: A gentle exercise that helps your body start to relax after a workout.

core: The muscles of your torso, including your abs and back muscles.

cross training: When an athlete trains for a sport she normally doesn't play, to exercise any muscle groups she might be weak in.

dehydration: When you don't have enough water in your body. When you exercise, you lose water by sweating, and it's important to replace it.

deltoids: The thick muscles covering your shoulder joint.

energy: The power your body needs to do things like move around and keep you alive.

endurance: The ability to keep going for a long time.

flexibility: How far you can bend, or how far your muscles can stretch.

glutes: Short for gluteals, the muscles in your buttocks.

hydration: Taking in more water to keep from getting dehydrated.

isometric: An exercise that you do without moving, by holding one position.

isotonic: An exercise you do by moving your muscles.

lactic acid: A chemical that builds up in your muscles after you exercise. It causes a burning feeling during anaerobic exercises.

lats: Short for latissimus dorsi, the large muscles along your back.

metabolism: How fast you digest food and burn energy.

muscle: The parts of your body that contract and expand to allow you to move.

nervous system: Made up of your brain, spinal cord, and nerves, which carry messages between your brain, spinal cord, and the rest of your body.

nutrition: The chemical parts of the food you eat that your body needs to survive and use energy.

obliques: The muscles to either side of your stomach, under your ribcage.

pecs: Short for pectorals, the muscles on your chest.

quads: Short for quadriceps, the large muscle on the front of your upper leg and thigh.

reps: How many times you repeat an anaerobic exercise in a row.

strength: The power of your muscles.

stretching: Pulling on your muscles to make them longer. Stretching before you exercise can keep you flexible and prevent injuries.

warm up: A light exercise you do before a workout to get your body ready for harder exercise.

weight training: Exercises that involve lifting heavy weights to increase your strength and endurance.

INDEX

ABOUT THE AUTHOR AND THE CONSULTANT

Z.B. Hill is an author and publicist living in Binghamton, NY. He has written books on a variety of topics including mental health, music, and fitness.

Diane H. Hart, Nationally Certified Fitness Professional and Health Specialist, has designed and implemented fitness and wellness programs for more than twenty years. She is a master member of the International Association of Fitness Professionals, and a health specialist for Blue Shield of Northeastern New York, HealthNow, and Palladian Health. In 2010, Diane was elected president of the National Association for Health and Fitness (NAHF), a nonprofit organization that exists to improve the quality of life for individuals in the United States through the promotion of physical fitness, sports, and healthy lifestyles. NAHF accomplishes this work by fostering and supporting state governors and state councils and coalitions that promote and encourage regular physical activity. NAHF is also the national sponsor of Employee Health and Fitness Month, the largest global workplace health and fitness event each May. American College of Sports Medicine (ACSM) has been a strategic partner with NAHF since 2009.

PICTURE CREDITS

MERIDIAN MIDDLE SCHOOL
2195 Brandywyn Lane
Buffalo Grove, IL 60089